To those who build satisfaction with their hands
and happiness with their heart

©knotmonsters.com

What started as something to pass the time during quarantine has turned into so much more. These toys bring me joy when I make them and even more when I give them away. I hope that my creations will bring you and your lucky loved ones hours of happiness as well. I want to give a special thanks to *YOU* for making my creations and bringing them to life. Your continued support encourages my creative side.

THANK YOU

NOTHING IS HARD, ONLY NEW

If you have never crocheted before, **NO PROBLEM**. Everyone has to start somewhere. When I first started, it took me a week just to figure out how to make a ball. It took even longer to get my fingers and hands used to holding a crochet hook. Crocheting can be frustrating at first but like with all things new, your body will develop muscle memory and over time, you will find that it will get easier. Always remember that nothing is hard, only new. There is no right way or wrong way to crochet. Whatever works for you, your body, and your ability is the right way. Some people will hold a crochet hook like a pen, I prefer to hold it like a knife, with my index finger along the length of the hook. This is purely personal preference. Crochet is an art form and like all art forms, is open to personal interpretation. Crochet patterns function as guidelines only, and I encourage you to bring your own artistic flair to each pattern. Do not be afraid to use different hooks or types of yarn. Experiment by changing the colors. Add accessories, modify the body shape, and bring your own individual spice to each pattern. Sometimes it will work; most of the time, it will not, and that is perfectly fine because in the end, you will end up with something that is yours. Something that you created. Your own little knotmonster.

1

HOOK, YARN, AND SINKER

Crocheting requires two fundamental things: a hook and yarn. Hook sizes are measured in millimeters and are also given a corresponding letter. For example, a 3.75mm hook is called an "F" hook and a 4mm hook is called a "G" hook. For amigurumi, I like to use a 3.75mm or a 4mm hook with worsted weight yarn. The smaller the hook, the tighter the stitches will be; the bigger the hook, the looser the stitches will be. The yarn is complementary to the hook. A thinner yarn will require a smaller hook, and a thicker yarn will require a larger one. Let's talk about what else you will need.

To start, you will need:

Hook [3.75mm (F) or 4mm (G)]

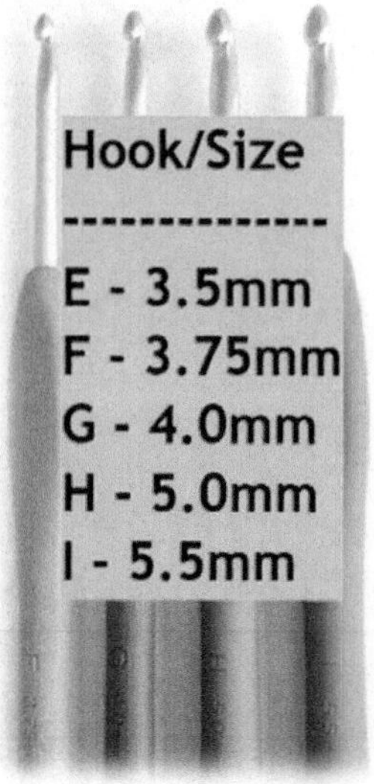

Yarn (worsted weight)

Scissors

Stitch marker (eg. scrap yarn, paper clip)

Safety eyes (8-14 mm)

Yarn needle #16 with blunt tip

Stuffing material

Pen/paper

Hook/Size

E - 3.5mm
F - 3.75mm
G - 4.0mm
H - 5.0mm
I - 5.5mm

Additional items:

Ruler

Hot glue or fabric glue

Felt (multiple colors)

Embroidery thread

Fabric scissors are specifically designed to cut fabric. They are incredibly sharp and will cut the yarn without fraying of the ends. This makes it much easier to thread the yarn through the needle when you are tying off.

Safety eyes are called "safety" because they have a small hole in the bottom of the eye. If a small child accidentally aspirates the eye, this hole will allow for air to pass through it. This is the concept, but it is not fool proof. Always use caution when you are giving a toy to a child under the age of three or to a child who tends to put things in their mouth. Alternatively, for these children, I would highly recommend making eyes out of yarn or felt instead. It is also important to thoroughly tie in your loose ends so your toys will not unravel and fall apart.

Stitch markers can be purchased from any craft store or online. Stitch markers help you keep track of where your first stitch in a row is. By marking your first stitch with a stitch marker, you will know when you have reached the end of your row. Alternatively, you can use a paper clip or a piece of scrap yarn (my personal favorite).

You want a needle that is wide enough to allow for worsted weight yarn to pass through the eye, while small enough to comfortably weave in your ends when you finish. A trick to easily thread your needle is to flatten the end of the yarn.

Accessories and pieces can be sewn or glued to your knotmonsters. Whenever possible, sew the pieces on, as they will hold much better than glue. However, glue works great to attach felt eyes as long as they are thoroughly attached, including the edges. When sewing, I recommend using the mattress stitch technique in order to hide the stitch as much as possible. For a mattress stitch, draw the yarn up one stitch and back down through the next stitch on the same piece. Then attach it to the other piece and repeat

2

HOW TO CROCHET

When you start a new pattern, the technique of crocheting will be noted as either completed in the straight or the round. Straight crocheting is completed in rows by going to the end of a row and turning around, creating a square-like pattern. Round crocheting is completed in rounds and, starting at the center, is done in spirals creating a circular pattern. Typically, a chain is used to start a straight crochet while a magic ring is used to start a round crochet. Exceptions to this are when an oval shape is desired. In this situation, you may form a chain and then, instead of turning at the end of the row, continuing onwards to the opposite side of the chain, thus creating an oval.

Patterns are written in different ways around the world. For example, in a UK pattern, a double crochet can mean a single crochet in a US pattern. For the sake of simplicity, all my patterns are based in US format and I have done my best to make them as simple and easy to read as possible. Each row/round is delineated by "R1, R2, R3, etc." When crocheting in the straight, at the end of each row, chain 1, turn the piece and start on the next row in the second chain from your hook. This step is necessary to create height in the piece. When crocheting in the round, one round means that you have crocheted completely around and have returned to the first stitch that you placed from the previous round. No chain/turning is necessary when crocheting in the round using any of my patterns because we will be working in a spiral motion. At the end of each row/round you will see a (#). This number represents how many stitches you should end up with when you finish the row/round.

Let's do an example: "R3: (SC, inc) x 6 (18)"

This means that we are on round number three, and we will do a single crochet and then an increase; and then repeat that five more times. At the end of our round, we will end up with eighteen total stitches.

Difficulty is rated by easy, medium, or advanced, based on the number of unique stitch techniques in each pattern.

While standard crochet will work just fine for amigurumi patterns, I use cross stitching for all my amigurumi. Cross stitching tightens up the stitches and helps prevent the stuffing from showing and the stitches from stretching. It also makes a neat grid-like texture. Therefore, <u>the following tutorials are for cross stitching and not standard crochet</u>. If you are familiar with crocheting and notice that these instructions are backwards by yarning over instead of under, it is because of cross stitching. The patterns will look perfectly adorable if you decide to not use cross stitching.

Slipknot

A slip knot allows you to tighten the knot with the loose yarn end. To create a slipknot, pull a loop made of the loose yarn end through the top of the first loop and tighten the knot. Pull on the loose yarn end to tighten the loop.

Chain (ch)

Start with your hook around a slipknot. Yarn over (yarn is over the hook) and pull through. You have made one chain or "ch 1." To create multiple chains, continue yarning over until desired chain # is met.

Slip Stitch (sl)

Enter next stitch with hook. Yarn under (yarn is under the hook – note this is for cross stitch) and pull through both loops. When you get to future rows, for sl, SC, DC, and TC, be sure to insert your hook under both loops when you start.

Single Crochet (SC)

Enter next stitch with hook. Yarn under (yarn is under the hook – note this is for cross stitch) and pull through first loop. Yarn over, pull through both loops.

KnotMonster
Single Crochet

Half Double Crochet (HDC)

Yarn over, enter next stitch with hook. Yarn under (yarn is under the hook – note this is for cross stitch) and pull through all three loops.

Double Crochet (DC)

Yarn over, enter next stitch with hook. Yarn under (yarn is under the hook – note this is for cross stitch) and pull through first two loops. Yarn over and pull through last two loops.

KnotMonster
Double Crochet

11

Triple Crochet (TC)

Yarn over twice, enter next stitch with hook. Yarn under (yarn is under the hook – note this is for cross stitch) and pull through first two loops. Yarn over and pull through next two loops. Yarn over and pull through last two loops.

Increase (inc)

Single crochet twice in the same stitch.

Invisible Decrease (dec)

While not completely invisible and the name may suggest, the goal of an invisible decrease is to reduce the number of stitches in a row while creating minimal seams. This is done by inserting the hook into the next stitch. Then insert the hook into the following stitch. These stitches will be the front loops facing you on subsequent rows. Yarn under (note this is for cross stitch) and pull through first two loops. Then yarn over and pull through both loops.

Magic Ring

Position fingers and yarn as shown in (1), grab yarn from underneath loose end (2), twist (3), yarn over (4), pull through (5). You will not have a slipknot on a loop, so if you pull on the loose end the loop will close. Single crochet six times into the ring (9) and tighten up the loop (10). This will create a magic ring 6 (MR 6) which is the most common start to most amigurumi.

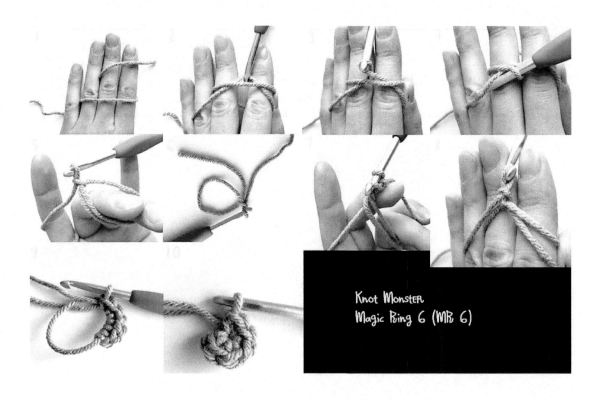

Knot Monster
Magic Ring 6 (MR 6)

Front loops only (FLO) & Back loops only (BLO)

When a pattern calls for **FLO** or **BLO**, this means that you will be doing the next row in the back or the front loops only. If the next row does not indicate FLO/BLO, then switch back to normal crochet under both loops. Back and front is relative to you, so if the loop is facing you then that is the front loop and vice versa.

Switching colors

To change colors, when you reach the next row, draw up the new color through both loops and then single crochet into the next stitch. Tie both loose ends together in the back of the project.

Puff Stitch

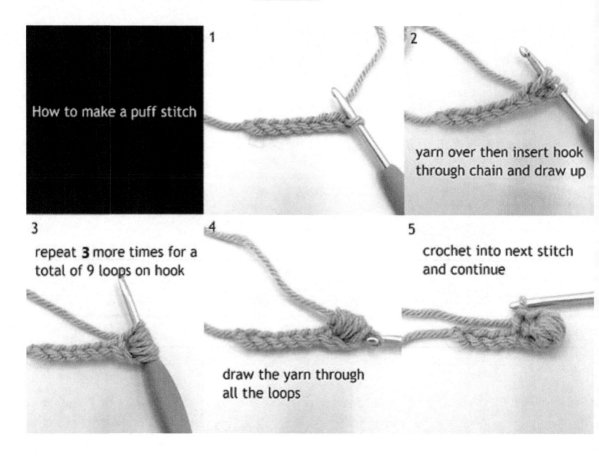

1 How to make a puff stitch

2 yarn over then insert hook through chain and draw up

3 repeat **3** more times for a total of 9 loops on hook

4 draw the yarn through all the loops

5 crochet into next stitch and continue

Oval Shape

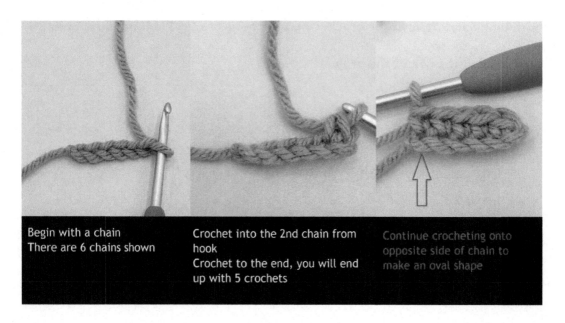

Begin with a chain
There are 6 chains shown

Crochet into the 2nd chain from hook
Crochet to the end, you will end up with 5 crochets

Continue crocheting onto opposite side of chain to make an oval shape

Attaching two feet together

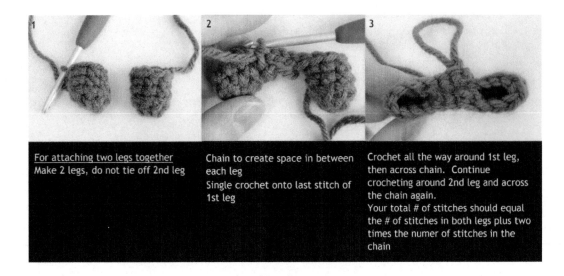

1 For attaching two legs together
Make 2 legs, do not tie off 2nd leg

2 Chain to create space in between each leg
Single crochet onto last stitch of 1st leg

3 Crochet all the way around 1st leg, then across chain. Continue crocheting around 2nd leg and across the chain again.
Your total # of stitches should equal the # of stitches in both legs plus two times the numer of stitches in the chain

Tying off

When you reach the end of your project. To tie off, slip stitch into the next stitch, then chain one. Pull the yarn all the way through, leaving a long end for sewing and cut the yarn where the red arrow is. Thread the yarn through a #16 yarn needle and weave it through several nearby stitches. Do this in three separate directions and then pass the yarn through the project and cut the yarn to hide the loose end.

Burger

Difficulty: Easy

Hook: 4.0mm (G) or 3.75 mm (F) hook

Approximate size: 8cm x 8cm

Eye: 6 mm

<u>All rows completed in the round unless otherwise indicated</u>

BUN

Part 1

Start with color brown

R1: MR 6 (6)

R2: inc x 6 (12)

R3: (SC, inc) x 6 (18)

R4: (SC 2, inc) x 6 (24)

R5: (SC 3, inc) x 6 (30)

R6: (SC 4, inc) x 6 (36)

R7: (SC 5, inc) x 6 (42)

R8: (SC 6, inc) x 6 (48)

R9-12: SC 48 (48)

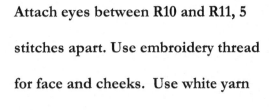

Attach eyes between R10 and R11, 5 stitches apart. Use embroidery thread for face and cheeks. Use white yarn for sesame seeds.

Change color to light brown

R13: BLO (SC 6, dec) x 6 (42)

R14: (SC 5, dec) x 6 (36)

R15: (SC 4, dec) x 6 (30)

R16: (SC 3, dec) x 6 (24)

R17: (SC 2, dec) x 6 (18)

Stuff very lightly

R18: (SC, dec) x 6 (12)

R19: dec x 6 (6)

Tie off

19

Part 2

Start with color brown

R1: MR 6 (6)

R2: inc x 6 (12)

R3: (SC, inc) x 6 (18)

R4: (SC 2, inc) x 6 (24)

R5: (SC 3, inc) x 6 (30)

R6: (SC 4, inc) x 6 (36)

R7: (SC 5, inc) x 6 (42)

R8: (SC 6, inc) x 6 (48)

R9: BLO SC 48 (48)

R10: SC 48 (48)

Change color to light brown

R11: BLO (SC 6, dec) x 6 (42)

R12: (SC 5, dec) x 6 (36)

R13: (SC 4, dec) x 6 (30)

R14: (SC 3, dec) x 6 (24)

R15: (SC 2, dec) x 6 (18)

Stuff very lightly

R16: (SC, dec) x 6 (12)

R17: dec x 6 (6)

Tie off

Sun's out
Buns out

PATTY

Start with color brown

R1: MR 6 (6)

R2: inc x 6 (12)

R3: (SC, inc) x 6 (18)

R4: (SC 2, inc) x 6 (24)

R5: (SC 3, inc) x 6 (30)

R6: (SC 4, inc) x 6 (36)

R7: (SC 5, inc) x 6 (42)

R8: (SC 6, inc) x 6 (48)

R9: SC 48 (48)

R10: (SC 6, dec) x 6 (42)

R11: (SC 5, dec) x 6 (36)

R12: (SC 4, dec) x 6 (30)

R13: (SC 3, dec) x 6 (24)

R14: (SC 2, dec) x 6 (18)

R15: (SC, dec) x 6 (12)

R16: dec x 6 (6)

Tie off, do not stuff

CHEESE

Start with color yellow

Crocheted in the straight

*At the end of each row, chain 1, turn and your next stitch is completed in 2nd stitch from hook

Ch 17, turn, start in 2nd chain from hook

R1-17: SC 16 (16)

Tie off, sew in loose ends

TOMATO

Start with color red

R1: MR 6 (6)

R2: inc x 6 (12)

R3: (SC, inc) x 6 (18)

R4: (SC 2, inc) x 6 (24)

R5: (SC 3, inc) x 6 (30)

R6: (SC 4, inc) x 6 (36)

R7: (SC 2, inc, SC 3) x 6 (42)

Tie off, sew in loose ends

LETTUCE

Start with color green

R1: MR 6 (6)

R2: inc x 6 (12)

R3: (SC, inc) x 6 (18)

R4: (SC 2, inc) x 6 (24)

R5: (SC 3, inc) x 6 (30)

R6: (SC 4, inc) x 6 (36)

R7: (3 DC's in each stitch) x 36 (108)

Tie off, sew in loose ends

French Fries

Difficulty: Easy

Hook: 4.0mm (G) or 3.75 mm (F) hook

Approximate size: 10cm x 10cm

Eye: 6 mm

<u>**All rows completed in the round unless otherwise indicated**</u>

<u>BOX</u>

Start with color red

Ch 14, turn and begin in 2nd chain from hook

R1: SC 13, continue onto other side of chain SC 13 (26)

R2: inc, SC 11, inc x 2, SC 11, inc (30)

R3: SC, inc, SC 11, (SC, inc) x 2, SC 12, inc (34)

R4: BLO SC 34 (34)

R5-14: SC 34 (34)

R15: SC 4, ch 1, turn, starting in 2nd chain from hook: SC 24 (24)

R16-17: ch 1, turn, starting in 2nd chain from hook: SC 24 (24)

Ch 1, tie off

Attach eyes between R22 and R23, 5 stitches apart. Use embroidery thread for face and cheeks.

24

FRIES

Part 1 (make 5) – back row

Start with color yellow

R1: MR 6 (6)

R2-19: SC 6 (6)

Tie off, do not stuff

Part 2 (make 2) – front row

Start with color yellow

R1: MR 6 (6)

R2-15: SC 6 (6)

Tie off, do not stuff

Part 3 (make 2) – front row

Start with color yellow

R1: MR 6 (6)

R2-16: SC 6 (6)

Tie off, do not stuff

Time fries when
I'm with you

KETCHUP/MUSTARD

Tie off, place inside part 1

Part 1

Start with color white

R1: MR 6 (6)

R2: inc x 6 (12)

R3: (SC, inc) x 6 (18)

R4: BLO SC 18 (18)

R5-8: SC 18 (18)

Tie off

Part 2

Use color red (for ketchup) **and** *yellow*

(for mustard)

R1: MR 6 (6)

R2: inc x 6 (12)

R3: BLO SC 12 (12)

R4-5: SC 12 (12)

Stuff

R6: BLO dec x 6 (6)

26

Soda Cup

Difficulty: Easy

Hook: 4.0mm (G) or 3.75 mm (F) hook

Approximate size: 15cm x 10cm

Eye: 8 mm

All rows completed in the round unless otherwise indicated

BODY

Start with color white

R1: MR 6 (6)

R2: inc x 6 (12)

R3: (SC, inc) x 6 (18)

R4: (SC 2, inc) x 6 (24)

R5: (SC 3, inc) x 6 (30)

R6: (SC 4, inc) x 6 (36)

Change color to red

R7: BLO SC 36 (36)

R8-9: SC 36 (36)

R10: (SC 11, inc) x 3 (39)

R11-13: SC 39 (39)

R14: (SC 6, inc, SC 6) x 3 (42)

R15-17: SC 42 (42)

R18: (SC 13, inc) x 4 (45)

R19-21: SC 45 (45)

R22: (SC 7, inc, SC 7) x 3 (48)

R23-25: SC 48 (48)

Change to color brown

R26: BLO (SC 6, dec) x 6 (42)

R27: (SC 5, dec) x 6 (36)

R28: (SC 4, dec) x 6 (30)

R29: (SC 3, dec) x 6 (24)

Stuff, attach eyes. Use embroidery thread for face and cheeks.

R30: (SC 2, dec) x 6 (18)

R31: (SC, dec) x 6 (12)

Stuff, make sure top and bottom are flat

R32: dec x 6 (6)

Change color to red

R33: BLO SC 3, dec, SC (5)

R34-41: SC 5 (5)

Tie off, do not stuff straw

You are
Soda-lightful

Start with color white

R1: Ch 6, fold in circle and inc x 6 starting in first chain. This will leave a hole in the center for the straw

R2: (SC, inc) x 6 (18)

R3: (SC 2, inc) x 6 (24)

R4: (SC 3, inc) x 6 (30)

R5: (SC 4, inc) x 6 (36)

R6: (SC 5, inc) x 6 (42)

R7: (SC 6, inc) x 6 (48)

R8: (SC 4, inc, SC 3) x 6 (54)

R9: BLO SC 54 (54)

Tie off

29

Cheeseburger Sliders

Difficulty: Easy

Hook: 4.0mm (G) or 3.75 mm (F) hook

Approximate size: 5cm x 6cm

Eye: 6 mm

All rows completed in the round unless otherwise indicated

BODY

Start with color light brown

R1: MR 6 (6)

R2: inc x 6 (12)

R3: (SC, inc) x 6 (18)

R4: (SC 2, inc) x 6 (24)

R5: (SC 3, inc) x 6 (30)

R6: (SC 4, inc) x 6 (36)

R7-8: SC 36 (36)

Attach eyes between R6 and R7, 5 stitches apart. Use embroidery thread for face and cheeks.

Change color to yellow

R9: BLO SC 36 (36)

Change to color dark brown

R10: FLO (SC 5, inc) x 6 (42)

R11: SC 42 (42)

Change to color light brown

R12: BLO (SC 5, dec) x 6 (36)

R13: SC 36 (36)

R14: BLO (SC 4, dec) x 6 (30)

R15: (SC 3, dec) x 6 (24)

R16: (SC 2, dec) x 6 (18)

Stuff

R17: (SC, dec) x 6 (12)

R18: dec x 6 (6)

Tie off

> I'm into fitness...
> ...fitness cheeseburger into my mouth

Ketchup/Mustard

Difficulty: Easy

Hook: 4.0mm (G) or 3.75 mm (F) hook

Approximate size: 10cm x 6cm

Eye: 6 mm

<u>All rows completed in the round
unless otherwise indicated</u>

*Ketchup will be in color red, mustard
will be in color yellow*

BODY

Start with color red

R1: MR 6 (6)

R2: inc x 6 (12)

R3: (SC, inc) x 6 (18)

R4: (SC 2, inc) x 6 (24)

R5: (SC 3, inc) x 6 (30)

R6: BLO SC 30 (30)

R7-26: SC 30 (30) – stuff as you go

Attach eyes between R21 and R22, 5
stitches apart. Use embroidery thread
for mouth and cheeks.

R27: BLO (SC 3, dec) x 6 (24)

R28: (SC 2, dec) x 6 (18)

R29: FLO SC 18 (18)

R30: BLO SC 18 (18)

Stuff

R31: BLO dec x 9 (9)

R32: FLO (SC, dec) x 3 (6)

R33: SC 6 (6)

R34: (SC, dec) x 2 (4)

Tie off

I relish the fact
that you've mustard
the strength to
ketchup with me

©knotmonsters.com

Corndog

Difficulty: Easy

Hook: 4.0mm (G) or 3.75 mm (F) hook

Approximate size: 15cm x 5cm

Eye: 6 mm

<u>All rows completed in the round unless otherwise indicated</u>

BODY

Start with color brown

R1: MR 6 (6)

R2: inc x 6 (12)

R3: (SC, inc) x 6 (18)

R4: (SC 2, inc) x 6 (24)

R5-24: SC 24 (24)

Attach eyes between R22 and R23, 5 stitches apart. Use embroidery thread for face and cheeks.

Stuff

R25: (SC 2, dec) x 6 (18)

R26: (SC, dec) x 6 (12)

R27: dec x 6 (6)

R28-33: SC 6 (6) – stuff firmly as you go

Tie off

KETCHUP/MUSTARD

Use red or dark yellow yarn

Ch 20, leave ends long at beginning and end and sew to body

I know it's corny but you're my dog!

Pretzel

Difficulty: Easy

Hook: 4.0mm (G) or 3.75 mm (F) hook

Approximate size: 15cm x 10cm

Eye: 6 mm

<u>All rows completed in the round</u>
<u>unless otherwise indicated</u>

<u>BODY</u>

Start with color brown

R1: MR 6 (6)

R2: inc x 6 (12)

R3-127: SC 12 (12) -stuff as you go

Attach eyes after R4 and R9, use

embroidery thread for mouth and

cheeks

R128: dec x 6 (6)

Tie off, fold as shown by photo and

sew together.

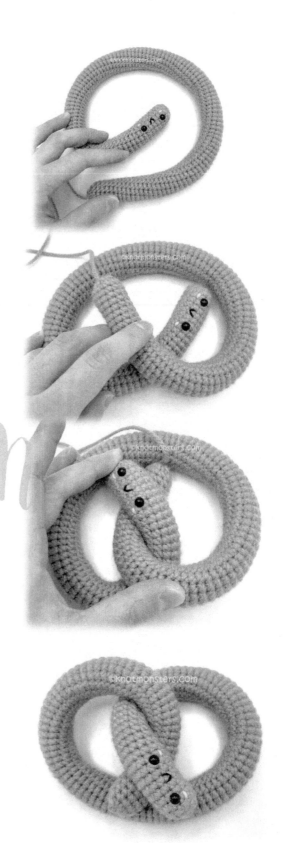

SALT

Start with color white

Draw yarn through a stitch on the pretzel and ch 1. Place one SC into same stitch. Tie off and sew in loose ends.

I'm knots about you

38

Cola Bottle

Difficulty: Easy

Hook: 4.0mm (G) or 3.75 mm (F) hook

Approximate size: 15cm x 6cm

Eye: 6 mm

All rows completed in the round unless otherwise indicated

BODY

Start with color brown

R1: MR 6 (6)

R2: inc x 6 (12)

R3: (SC, inc) x 6 (18)

R4: (SC 2, inc) x 6 (24)

R5: (SC 3, inc) x 6 (30)

R6: BLO SC 30 (30)

R7: (SC 8, dec) x 3 (27)

R8-9: SC 27 (27)

R10: (SC 7, dec) x 3 (24)

R11-13: SC 24 (24)

R14: (SC 7, inc) x 3 (27)

R15-16: SC 27 (27)

R17: (SC 8, inc) x 3 (30)

Change color to white

R18: SC 30 (30)

Change color to red

R19-22: SC 30 (30)

R23: (SC 8, dec) x 3 (27)

R24: SC 27 (27)

Change color to white

R25: (SC 7, dec) x 3 (24)

Change color to brown

R26: SC 24 (24)

Attach eyes between R22 and R23, 5 stitches apart. Use embroidery thread for face and cheeks. Stuff.

R27: (SC 6, dec) x 3 (21)

R28: SC 21 (21)

R29: (SC 5, dec) x 3 (18)

R30: SC 18 (18)

R31: (SC 4, dec) x 3 (15)

R32: SC 15 (15)

R33: (SC 3, dec) x 3 (12)

R34: SC 12 (12)

Switch color to gray

R35: FLO (SC, inc) x 6 (18)

Stuff

R36: BLO (SC, dec) x 6 (12)

R37: dec x 6 (6)

Tie off

Let's get fizzicle!

Pizza Slice

Difficulty: Advanced (colorwork required)

Hook: 4.0mm (G) or 3.75 mm (F) hook

Approximate size: 10cm x 10cm

Eye: 6 mm

All rows completed in the round unless otherwise indicated

BODY

Start with color brown

Ch 21, turn and begin in 2nd chain from hook

R1: SC 20, continue onto other side of chain SC 20 (40)

R2: inc, SC 18, inc x 2, SC 18, inc (44)

R3-4: SC 44 (44)

R5: dec, SC 18, dec x 2, SC 18, dec (40)

R6: SC 40 (40)

R7: (BLO for just this red section - *Change color to red*, SC 20), *change color to brown*, SC 20 (40)

R8: *Change color to yellow*, dec, SC 16, dec, *change color to brown*, dec, SC 16, dec (36)

R9-10: *Change color to yellow*, SC 18, *change color to brown*, SC 18 (36)

Stuff pizza lightly as you go. Attach eyes after R4 and R5, 5 stitches apart, use embroidery thread for mouth and cheeks.

R11: *Change color to yellow*, dec, SC 14, dec, *change color to brown*, dec, SC 14, dec (32)

R12-13: *Change color to yellow*, SC 16, *change color to brown*, SC 16 (32)

R14: *Change color to yellow*, dec, SC 12, dec, *change color to brown*, dec, SC 12, dec (28)

R15-16: *Change color to yellow*, SC 14, *change color to brown*, SC 14 (28)

R17: *Change color to yellow*, dec, SC 10, dec, *change color to brown*, dec, SC 10, dec (24)

R18-19: *Change color to yellow*, SC 12, *change color to brown*, SC 12 (24)

R20: *Change color to yellow*, dec, SC 8, dec, *change color to brown*, dec, SC 8, dec (20)

R21-22: *Change color to yellow*, SC 10, *change color to brown*, SC 10 (20)

R23: *Change color to yellow*, dec, SC 6, dec, *change color to brown*, dec, SC 6, dec (16)

R24-25: *Change color to yellow*, SC 8, *change color to brown*, SC 8 (16)

R26: *Change color to yellow*, dec, SC 4, dec, *change color to brown*, dec, SC 4, dec (12)

R27-28: *Change color to yellow*, SC 6, *change color to brown*, SC 6 (12)

R29: *Change color to yellow*, dec, SC 2, dec, *change color to brown*, dec, SC 2, dec (8)

R30: *Change color to yellow*, dec x 2, *change color to brown*, dec x 2 (4)

Tie off

Pepperoni (make 3)

Start with color red

R1: MR 6 (6)

R2: inc x 6 (12)

Tie off, attach to pizza

You got a pizza
my heart ♡

Hotdog & Bun

Difficulty: Easy

Hook: 4.0mm (G) or 3.75 mm (F) hook

Approximate size: 10cm x 6cm

Eye: 6 mm

All rows completed in the round unless otherwise indicated

HOTDOG

Start with color red

R1: MR 6 (6)

R2: inc x 6 (12)

R3: dec, SC 4, inc, SC 5 (12)

R4-7: SC 12 (12)

Stuff

R8: dec, SC 4, inc, SC 5 (12)

R9-18: SC 12 (12)

Stuff

R19: SC, inc, SC 4, dec, SC 4 (12)

R20-23: SC 12 (12)

Stuff

R24: SC, inc, SC 4, dec, SC 4 (12)

Stuff

R25: dec x 6 (6)

Tie off

To make mustard, use dark yellow yarn and ch 30, leave ends long at beginning and end for sewing to hotdog

47

BUN (make 2)

Start with color brown

R1: Ch 16, turn and starting in 2nd chain from hook SC 15. Continue around chain and SC 15. You should end up with 30 SC's (30)

R2: inc, SC 13, inc x 2, SC 13, inc (34)

R3: inc x 2, SC 13, inc x 4, SC 13, inc x 2 (42)

R4: (SC, inc) x 2, SC 13, (SC, inc) x 4, SC 13, (SC, inc) x 2 (50)

R5-6: SC 50 (50)

Change color to light brown

R7: BLO (SC, dec) x 2, SC 13, (SC, dec) x 4, SC 13, (SC, dec) x 2 (42)

If desired, attach eyes and use embroidery thread for mouth and cheeks

R8: dec x 2, SC 13, dec x 4, SC 13, dec x 2 (34)

R9: dec, SC 13, dec x 2, SC 13, dec (30)

Tie off, stuff lightly, sew closed.

Using brown yarn, sew together both pieces.

Sew hotdog inside of bun

Frank you very much for being the only bun for me

Curly Fries, Onion Rings, Chicken Nuggets, Mozzarella Sticks

Difficulty: Easy

Hook: 4.0mm (G) or 3.75 mm (F) hook

Approximate size: Tray measures 10 cm x 8 cm

Eye: 6 mm

<u>**All rows completed in the round unless otherwise indicated**</u>

TRAY

Start with color white

Ch 15, turn and begin in 2nd chain from hook

R1: SC 14, continue onto other side of chain SC 14 (28)

*(SC 3) = 3 SC's in 1 stitch

R2: (SC 3), SC 12, (SC 3) x 2, SC 12, (SC 3) (36)

R3: SC, (SC 3), SC 14, (SC 3), SC 2, (SC 3), SC 14, (SC 3), SC (44)

R4: SC 2, (SC 3), SC 16, (SC 3), SC 4, (SC 3), SC 16, (SC 3), SC 2 (52)

R5: SC 3, (SC 3), SC 18, (SC 3), SC 6, (SC 3), SC 18, (SC 3), SC 3 (60)

R6: BLO SC 60 (60)

R7-11: SC 60 (60) – if striped basket is desired, alternate between red and white colors from R7-11

Tie off

CURLY FRIES (make 3)

Start with color dark yellow

Ch 31, turn and begin in 2nd chain from hook. Crochet 3 SC's in each stitch.

ONION RINGS (make 3)

Start with color dark yellow

R1: MR 6 (6)

R2-25: SC 6 (6)

Tie off, do not stuff. Bend in a circle

and sew together.

MOZZARELLA STICKS

Version 1

Start with color dark yellow

R1: MR 6 (6)

R2: inc x 6 (12)

R3-17: SC 12 (12) -stuff as you go

Tie off

Version 2

Start with color dark yellow

R1: MR 6 (6)

R2: inc x 6 (12)

R3-7: SC 12 (12)

Stuff

Change color to off-white

R8: dec x 6 (6)

R9: BLO SC 6 (6)

R10-12: SC 6 (6)

Change color to dark yellow

R13: FLO inc x 6 (12)

R14-18: SC 12 (12)

Stuff

R19: dec x 6 (6)

Tie off

R9: dec, SC 8, inc, SC 7 (18)

R10: SC 18 (18)

R11: dec, SC 8, inc, SC 7 (18)

R12: SC 18 (18)

R13: dec, SC 5, dec x 2, SC 5, dec (14)

Stuff, sew closed

CHICKEN NUGGETS (make 3)

Start with color light brown

Ch 8, turn and begin in 2ⁿᵈ chain from hook

R1: SC 7, continue onto other side of chain SC 7 (14)

R2: inc, SC 5, inc x 2, SC 5, inc (18)

R3: SC 18 (18)

R4: inc, SC 8, dec, SC 7 (18)

R5: SC 18 (18)

R6: inc, SC 8, dec, SC 7 (18)

R7-8: SC 18 (18)

Taco

Difficulty: Easy

Hook: 4.0mm (G) or 3.75 mm (F) hook

Approximate size: 11cm x 6cm

Eye: 6 mm

<u>All rows completed in the round</u>
<u>unless otherwise indicated</u>

<u>SHELL</u>

Start with color yellow/brown

Ch 11, turn and begin in 2nd chain from hook

R1: SC 10, continue onto other side of chain SC 10 (20)

R2: inc, SC 7, inc x 3, SC 7, inc x 2 (26)

R3: SC, inc, SC 7, (SC, inc) x 3, SC 7, (SC, inc) x 2 (32)

R4: SC 2, inc, SC 7, (SC 2, inc) x 3, SC 7, (SC 2, inc) x 2 (38)

R5: SC 3, inc, SC 7, (SC 3, inc) x 3, SC 7, (SC 3, inc) x 2 (44)

R6: SC 4, inc, SC 7, (SC 4, inc) x 3, SC 7, (SC 4, inc) x 2 (50)

R7: SC 5, inc, SC 7, (SC 5, inc) x 3, SC 7, (SC 5, inc) x 2 (56)

R8: SC 6, inc, SC 7, (SC 6, inc) x 3, SC 7, (SC 6, inc) x 2 (62)

R9: SC 7, inc, SC 7, (SC 7, inc) x 3, SC 7, (SC 7, inc) x 2 (68)

R10: SC 8, inc, SC 7, (SC 8, inc) x 3, SC 7, (SC 8, inc) x 2 (74)

R11: SC 4, inc, SC 16, (inc, SC 9) x 2, inc, SC 16, inc, SC 9, inc, SC 5 (80)

Tie off, leave end long. Attach eyes and use embroidery thread for face and cheeks.

MEAT

Start with color brown

R1: MR 6 (6)

R2: inc x 6 (12)

R3: (SC, inc) x 6 (18)

R4-25: SC 18 (18) - stuff as you go

R26: (SC, dec) x 6 (12)

Stuff

R27: dec x 6 (6)

Tie off

SALSA

Start with color red

Ch 7, turn and begin in 2nd chain from hook

R1: SC 6, continue onto other side of chain SC 6 (12)

R2-21: SC 12 (12)

Tie off, sew closed. Do not stuff.

Attach to meat.

LETTUCE

Start with color green

Ch 16, turn and begin in 2nd chain from hook

R1: SC 15, continue onto other side of chain SC 15 (30)

R2: (3 DC's in each stitch) x 30 (90)

Tie off, attach to salsa and use long end from the shell to attach pieces together.

Let's taco bout how much I love tacos

56

Chips, Guacamole, and Salsa

Difficulty: Advanced

Hook: 4.0mm (G) or 3.75 mm (F) hook

Approximate size: 10cm x 5cm

Eye: 8 mm

<u>**All rows completed in the round unless otherwise indicated**</u>

CHIPS

Start with color yellow

Ch 11, turn and begin in 2nd chain from hook

R1: SC 10, continue onto other side of chain SC 10 (20)

R2: SC 20 (20)

R3: dec, SC 8, dec, SC 8 (18)

R4: dec, SC 7, dec, SC 7 (16)

R5: SC 16 (16)

R6: dec, SC 6, dec, SC 6 (14)

R7: dec, SC 5, dec, SC 5 (12)

R8: dec, SC 4, dec, SC 4 (10)

R9: dec, SC 3, dec, SC 4 (8)

R10: dec, SC 2, dec, SC 2 (6)

Tie off, do not stuff

I value our friend-chip

GUACAMOLE BOWL

Part 1

Start with color dark grey

R1: MR 6 (6)

R2: inc x 6 (12)

R3: (SC, inc) x 6 (18)

R4: (SC 2, inc) x 6 (24)

R5: (SC 3, inc) x 6 (30)

R6: (SC 4, inc) x 6 (36)

R7: (SC 5, inc) x 6 (42)

R8: (SC 6, inc) x 6 (48)

R9: (SC 7, inc) x 6 (54)

R10-21: SC 54 (54)

If desired, for face attach eyes. Use embroidery thread for mouth and cheeks.

R22: (SC 7, dec) x 6 (48)

R23: (SC 6, dec) x 6 (42)

R24: (SC 5, dec) x 6 (36)

R25: (SC 4, dec) x 6 (30)

Do not stuff, we will be inverting to create a bowl.

R26: (SC 3, dec) x 6 (24)

R27: (SC 2, dec) x 6 (18)

R28: (SC, dec) x 6 (12)

R29: dec x 6 (6)

Tie off, invert to create bowl shape

Part 2 – legs (make 3)

Start with color dark grey

Ch 7, turn and begin in 2nd chain from hook

R1: SC 6, continue onto other side of chain SC 6 (12)

R2-3: SC 12 (12)

Tie off, leave end long and sew to

bottom of part 1.

Part 3 – Guacamole

Start with color green

R1: MR 6 (6)

R2: inc x 6 (12)

R3: (SC, inc) x 6 (18)

R4: (SC 2, inc) x 6 (24)

R5: (SC 3, inc) x 6 (30)

R6: (SC 4, inc) x 6 (36)

R7: (SC 5, inc) x 6 (42)

R8: (puff, SC, puff, SC, puff, dec) x 6 (36)

R9: (SC, puff, SC, puff, dec) x 6 (30)

R10: (puff, SC, puff, dec) x 6 (24)

R11: (SC, puff, dec) x 6 (18)

Stuff

R12: (puff, dec) x 6 (12)

R13: dec x 6 (6)

Tie off

SALSA BOWL

Part 1

Start with color tan

R1: MR 6 (6)

R2: inc x 6 (12)

R3: (SC, inc) x 6 (18)

R4: (SC 2, inc) x 6 (24)

R5: (SC 3, inc) x 6 (30)

R6: BLO SC 30 (30)

R7: (SC 4, inc) x 6 (36)

R8: (SC 5, inc) x 6 (42)

R9: (SC 6, inc) x 6 (48)

R10: SC 48 (48)

Change color to yellow

R11: SC 48 (48)

Change color to green

R12: SC 48 (48)

Change color to tan

R13-17: SC 48 (48)

If desired, for face attach eyes. Use embroidery thread for mouth and cheeks.

R18: (SC 6, dec) x 6 (42)

R19: (SC 5, dec) x 6 (36)

R20: (SC 4, dec) x 6 (30)

Do not stuff, we will be inverting to create a bowl.

R21: (SC 3, dec) x 6 (24)

R22: (SC 2, dec) x 6 (18)

R23: (SC, dec) x 6 (12)

R24: dec x 6 (6)

Tie off, invert to create bowl shape

Part 2 - salsa

Start with color dark red

R1: MR 6 (6)

R2: inc x 6 (12)

R3: (SC, inc) x 6 (18)

R4: (SC 2, inc) x 6 (24)

R5: (SC 3, inc) x 6 (30)

R6: (SC 4, inc) x 6 (36)

R7: (SC 4, dec) x 6 (30)

R8: (puff, SC, puff, dec) x 6 (24)

R9: (SC 2, dec) x 6 (18)

Stuff

R10: (puff, dec) x 6 (12)

R11: dec x 6 (6)

Tie off

Bucket of Fried Chicken

Difficulty: Moderate

Hook: 4.0mm (G) or 3.75 mm (F) hook

Approximate size: 10cm x 10cm

Eye: 6 mm

**All rows completed in the round
unless otherwise indicated**

BUCKET

Start with color white

R1: MR 6 (6)

R2: inc x 6 (12)

R3: (SC, inc) x 6 (18)

R4: (SC 2, inc) x 6 (24)

R5: (SC 3, inc) x 6 (30)

R6: (SC 4, inc) x 6 (36)

R7: (SC 5, inc) x 6 (42)

R8: (SC 6, inc) x 6 (48)

R9: (SC 7, inc) x 6 (54)

R10: BLO SC 54 (54)

R11-20: SC 54 (54)

Change color to red

R21: SC 54 (54)

Change color to white

R22: SC 54 (54)

Change color to red

R23: SC 54 (54)

Change color to white

R24: SC 54 (54)

Tie off

63

CHICKEN DRUMSTICK (VER 1)

Start with color brown

R1: MR 6 (6)

R2: inc x 6 (12)

R3: (SC, inc) x 6 (18)

R4-5: SC 18 (18)

R6: (SC, dec) x 6 (12)

R7-8: SC 12 (12)

Stuff

R9: (SC 3, inc) x 3 (15)

R10: SC 15 (15)

R11: (SC 4, inc) x 3 (18)

R12: SC 18 (18)

R13: (SC 5, inc) x 3 (21)

R14: SC 21 (21)

R15: (SC 6, inc) x 3 (24)

R16: SC 24 (24)

R17: (SC 7, inc) x 3 (27)

R18: SC 27 (27)

R19: (SC 8, inc) x 3 (30)

R20: SC 30 (30)

R21: (SC 3, dec) x 6 (24)

Stuff, attach eyes. Use embroidery thread for face and cheeks.

R22: (SC 2, dec) x 6 (18)

R23: (SC, dec) x 6 (12)

Finish stuffing

R24: dec x 6 (6)

Tie off

CHICKEN DRUMSTICK (VER 2)

Part 1

Start with color white

R1: MR 6 (6)

R2: inc x 6 (12)

R3: SC 12 (12)

Tie off, set aside

Part 2

Start with color white

R1: MR 6 (6)

R2: inc x 6 (12)

R3: SC 12 (12)

R4: Connect parts 1 and 2 by single crocheting to last stitch of part 1. Single crochet all the way around the part 1, then continue crocheting around the part 2. Your total # of stitches will be 24. (24)

R5: dec x 12 (12)

There will be a stray end of yarn in the middle from the tail of the 2nd part, tie this off. Stuff.

R6: (SC, dec) x 4 (8)

R7-8: SC 8 (8)

Stuff

Change color to brown

R9: FLO (SC, inc) x 4 (12)

R10: SC 12 (12)

R11: (SC 3, inc) x 3 (15)

R12: SC 15 (15)

R13: (SC 4, inc) x 3 (18)

R14: SC 18 (18)

R15: (SC 5, inc) x 3 (21)

R16: SC 21 (21)

R17: (SC 6, inc) x 3 (24)

R18: SC 24 (24)

Stuff

R19: (SC 7, inc) x 3 (27)

R20: SC 27 (27)

R21: (SC 8, inc) x 3 (30)

R22: SC 30 (30)

R23: (SC 3, dec) x 6 (24)

Stuff, attach eyes. Use embroidery

thread for face and cheeks.

R24: (SC 2, dec) x 6 (18)

R25: (SC, dec) x 6 (12)

Finish stuffing

R26: dec x 6 (6)

Tie off

My love for you is deep...fried!

67

Soda Can

Difficulty: Easy

Hook: 4.0mm (G) or 3.75 mm (F) hook

Approximate size: 9cm x 6cm

Eye: 8 mm

All rows completed in the round unless otherwise indicated

BODY

Start with color grey

R1: MR 6 (6)

R2: inc x 6 (12)

R3: (SC, inc) x 6 (18)

R4: (SC 2, inc) x 6 (24)

R5: (SC 3, inc) x 6 (30)

R6: (SC 4, inc) x 6 (36)

Change color to red

R7: BLO SC 36 (36)

R8-13: SC 36 (36)

Change color to white

R14-17: SC 36 (36)

Change color to red

R18-23: SC 36 (36)

Change color to grey

R24: BLO SC 36 (36)

R25: BLO (SC 4, dec) x 6 (30)

R26: (SC 3, dec) x 6 (24)

Stuff, attach eyes. Use embroidery thread for face and cheeks.

R27: (SC 2, dec) x 6 (18)

R28: (SC, dec) x 6 (12)

Stuff lightly, make sure top and bottom are flat

R29: dec x 6 (6)

Tie off

Let's get Fizzicle

68

TAB

Start with color grey

R1: MR 6 (6)

R2-5: SC 6 (6)

Tie off, do not stuff. Flatten and sew to top of can.

Movie Popcorn

Difficulty: Advanced

Hook: 4.0mm (G) or 3.75 mm (F) hook

Approximate size: 12cm x 8cm

Eye: 8 mm

All rows completed in the round unless otherwise indicated

BOX

Part 1 – this part is crocheted in the straight. At the end of each row, chain 1, turn and your next stitch is completed in 2nd stitch from hook

Start with color white

Ch 21, turn, start in 2nd chain from hook

R1-2: SC 20 (20)

Change to color red

R3-4: SC 20 (20)

Change to color white

R5-6: SC 20 (20)

Change to color red

R7-8: SC 20 (20)

Change to color white

R9-10: SC 20 (20)

Change to color red

R11-12: SC 20 (20)

Change to color white

R13-14: SC 20 (20)

Change to color red

R15-16: SC 20 (20)

Change to color white

R17-18: SC 20 (20)

Change to color red

R19-20: SC 20 (20)

Change to color white

R21-22: SC 20 (20)

Change to color red

R23-24: SC 20 (20)

Change to color white

R25-26: SC 20 (20)

Change to color red

R27-28: SC 20 (20)

There will be lots of loose ends but they will all be on the same side. Tie off loose ends. Fold in a circle and sew.

Part 2 - base

*(SC 3) = 3 SC's in 1 stitch

Start with color white

R1: MR 8 (8)

R2: [(SC 3), SC] x 4 (16)

R3: SC, [(SC 3), SC 3] x 3, (SC 3), SC 2 (24)

R4: SC 2, [(SC 3), SC 5] x 3, (SC 3), SC 3 (32)

R5: SC 3, [(SC 3), SC 7] x 3, (SC 3), SC 4 (40)

R6: SC 4, [(SC 3), SC 9] x 3, (SC 3), SC 5 (48)

R7: SC 5, [(SC 3), SC 11] x 3, (SC 3), SC 6 (56)

Tie off, single crochet all the way around part 1. Flip inside out. Place loose ends on the inside

POPCORN

Use 2 different shades of yellow

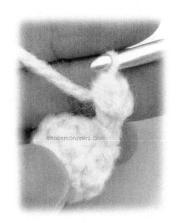

R1: MR 6 (6)

R2: inc x 6 (12)

R3: SC 12 (12)

Stuff

R4: dec x 6 (6)

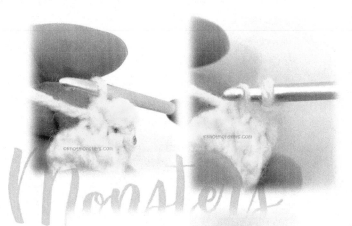

R5: [(ch 2, HDC in 2nd chain from hook), dec] x 3 (3)

Tie off

Hey! What's Poppin?

About the Author

Michael grew up in sunny Las Vegas, Nevada and currently works as a pediatric dentist. His favorite thing in the world is to make others smile, and he hopes his little stuffed creations will bring many more smiles all over the world.

Some fun facts about Michael: His favorite animal is a penguin. Favorite children's movie is "Elf." Favorite sport is roller skating. Favorite crochet pattern is his sunflower pattern. His fondest crochet memory is first starting crocheting and taking three days and many tears to make a crochet ball. A skill that most people do not know about is that he once stacked fifteen Cheerios. If he were a superhero, his superpower would be super speed. He can also recite the general prologue of The Canterbury Tales in old English, which has thus far proved completely useless ☺.